COLIN IS CHANGING HIS NAME

JOHN ANDREWS

SIBLING RIVALRY PRESS
LITTLE ROCK, ARKANSAS
DISTURB / ENRAPTURE

Colin Is Changing His Name
Copyright © 2017 by John Andrews

Cover art by Bradley Phillips:
"Untitled #3" from the series *The Space Between Words*
Author photograph by Randy Kitchens
Book design by Bryan Borland
Cover design by Seth Pennington

Sibling Rivalry Press, LLC
PO Box 26147
Little Rock, AR 72221

info@siblingrivalrypress.com

www.siblingrivalrypress.com

ISBN: 978-1-943977-35-2

Library of Congress Control No: 2017933049

This title is housed permanently in the Rare Books and Special Collections Vault of the Library of Congress.

First Sibling Rivalry Press Edition, June 2017

For John

I

II

III

I

SLEEPOVER

Rush to the part where we fear again
between footsteps and hall light switches,

force hush in our veins busy
to reverse hands on thighs.

Say the pledge of allegiance,
least sexy words you know:

collateral damage, atrophy,
terminal, any way to distract.

Movies about ghosts, room
after room of dark soup dust air.

Tuck our boners back between
legs. Make shadows on the walls

into men with knives for eyes, melon-baller
fingers that can scoop pulp faster

than a jack-o-lantern carving contest,
and a father at the door with an axe

ready to chop light across our bodies.

COLIN IS CHANGING HIS NAME

*

You don't have to be Colin,
Colin's mother says, there are
ways to erase things. Try on
a new name at camp.

There are so many better names
like Matthew, Logan, maybe
Richard. These things aren't
stone, but water. God can

wash you clean.

*

Sometimes, Colin fears
dying for being Colin.
So he wears the right shoes,
reconsiders his tie.

Sometimes the people
he passes on the street
know his name,
shout out the window,

Hey, Colin!

*

In a new place people always
ask what you want
to be called, if you have a
preferred name for paperwork.

In the doctor's office,
blue ink pools on the form.
Colin hesitates, there is so much
in what we let

others call us.

*

Colin says only other Colins
can call him Colin. Somehow
it hurts less coming from
a Colin, because Colins

took it back, wrote it between
"Hello, my name is"
and "how are you?"
in blue marker, wore it

beyond the meet and greet.

*

Colin kneels beside his bed,
asks every night for a new
name, says he's earned it,
says he's sorry for being

Colin. And the morning cracks
his window in half with light.
His room, always the same. His skin
still the suit he wore last night,

his letters, his name tag, his name.

ZONE OF SILENCE

Last night, I made a map of my bed,
sandbar where everything ends up
without cellphone reception.
I can hear you now,
crying in the bathroom.
The tile breaking against—
I kissed you.
I am sorry, I'll say it again.
St. Elmo's fire: sailors' swear
comes all at once, the sky
burning for something that isn't
there. I wanted to find something
at the end of the world. We lie,
strangers floating on soft
water stuck inside the bed.
The ocean is mostly made up of ash:
my grandmother, your uncle,
it doesn't matter who.

LOOKING FOR CONSTELLATIONS

trying to find
the one

where two brothers
wrapped

each other
like water moccasins

it is the only way
we could

see ourselves
in heaven

LITTLE ROCK RAIN

The moment he says
I am sorry.

We'll never get a high school

                          prom, first kiss.
   I bought that boutonnière
                for you, but gave it to—
Flowers die everyday.
So do young boys who fall
             for wrists,
       the way you held a trumpet.

I want to love you,
         but the city is on fire.
   Everyone, including me
      looked away, each time a boy
          had his chest checked like a truck tire.
     No one is meant to live
                like this: afraid to kiss. This is it.
   Everyone turns their back
           in the parking lot. Your chest holds more air,
      a man with a billy club wants
              to be sure,
I love you,
     but I can't—

APPROACHING INFINITY

Walk into a bar, any bar
you like. Tonight,
say it's the one
with broken neon
olive squinting in a martini glass.
You are Colin.

You meet Colin.
Say: *Hi Colin, I am Colin.*
Drink, dance, do all the things
that begin with the letter D.
Take Colin home.
Put two Colins in the well, take one out.

*

Try the park, a shaded park,
the one with graffiti and high
school kids after dark
with their fortys and smoke.
Ignore everyone as best you can
till you find Colin behind a bush.

Take Colin against a tree, carve your initials.
Say something from a movie
or don't, the outcome is the same;
there aren't forking paths to pick from
in these woods. There are two Colins,
put them in the well, take one out.

*

Go back to the same bar.
Meet another Colin, Colin
in a leather jacket. The kind of Colin
your father wouldn't like:
tattooed, tight jeaned,
and all Colin.

Take this Colin and make a map
of the known universe with your tongue.
Count the toes, fingers, match
the forms limb to limb, it's only rational
to see two without counting. Put the Colins in
the well, take one out.

*

Tired of bars and parks, you go grocery shopping.
Pause in the meat section. There isn't
a butcher anymore, just Colins.
Colin stocks the steaks
and you are sure he is
Colin from his name tag.

Follow Colin to the freezer.
We know where this goes,
Colin and Colin on a pile of meat.
Colin and Colin on a pile of Colin.
Colin and Colin at the edge of a well.
Colin and Colin and—

*

Tonight we'll try the college bar:
Colin in his tight shirt,
Colin with love dangling
from his mouth,
the Colin who doesn't
know he is Colin.

Standing in the middle
of the room as if buds bound
so tightly they could burst
into irises, tulips that command
attention. The well is full, but you can't help
but think of all the other Colins.

*

Let's remember middle
school where everything is sour
or sugar, it all depends
on the first Colin.
Kiss the right Colin
and you'll be invited to sleep over.

Kiss the wrong Colin
you'll lose your front teeth in the bathroom,
your dentist says this happens all the time:
young men break teeth.
Go back to the well,
look down at the Colins.

FOUR COLINS SHARE A BURRITO

Colin is Colin-fat,
which means his jeans
fit, but *should* be smaller.

There are too many calories for one
person to carry alone. Colin
offers to share everything

he eats with Twink Colin,
Colin who can eat and wash
his shirt on his chest.

It's harder to share with bear-
Colin, who doesn't count
content, bites off all

he likes while Colin-fat Colin talks
to his stomach about absence
and beauty. Twink-Colin knows pills

to forget hunger, sometimes
a pipe he calls the Crystal
Light diet. Colin

never knows what to call
himself, left alone
in front of a mirror.

SONG

between lungs
it's the
          same
     and not

like relearning to two step
               with a man
     when eyes close at
          separate speeds

your mouth is wine
          there isn't enough

          there is never enough

     someone will have to take
                    us home

your mouth is poison

     all the trees have to give
          up eventually

I love this
poem so fucking
much

PSYCHOPATHIA SEXUALIS

Colin 138:

Never took slightest notice
of opposite sex. At 24,
first time in a brothel,

took flight from
a nude female figure.
At 25, intercourse with men

of his own stamp.
For business reasons, married
a lady. By imagination

managed being potent
with his wife, who, at heart
he loved passionately.

When a child was born,
he withdrew out of fear
of procreating offspring

with his name.

Colin 147:

At the age of six, he began to feel
happy. In company of men,
blushed at the sight of beards,

dared not look at handsome
for fear of turning red
that would not fade.

Liked to go to balls,
not for the girls,
but fine gentlemen

thinking always he was
in their embrace.
At seventeen, seduced:

mutual masturbation,
delight, shame,
he recognized

the abnormality.

Colin 148:

First drawn to male persons,
then puberty set in, he fell
for his school teachers.

His dreams: pollutions,
always about men, shy
and confused like a maiden.

Even with an abundant
beard, decided masculinity,
he had the illusion

everyone noticed his want.
Music brought heavy
perspiration over his body.

Upon closer acquaintance
he showed. Without a vestige
of independence, gave

himself over.

Colin 149:

Preferring those in their 30s
with moustaches, his sexual needs
were extraordinary, erections frequent.

At the age of 12, began to fall
for men; but only 12 times
had he been successful

in this. Active as well
as passive pederasty disgusted
him. He never accepted

such offers. His love
for sympathetic men
was boundless. Coitus

did not please. Only
at the moment
of ejaculation

did he experience.

Colin 150:

Colleen on occasion,
24 and discovered.
The form of his face

was feminine, but
otherwise male.
Wore female

clothing since 14.
Long hair after
the manner of women,

parted in the middle.
Passed as an actress.
Beard carefully

pulled out, genitals
tucked back
artfully

bandaged.

Colin 151:

An official of middle
age, for some years
had been happy

in family life. Married
to a virtuous woman. Presented
manifestations of anti-pathic

sexual feeling. Through indiscretion,
a prostitute made public:
once a week,

would appear in a house
of false names, prancing
in silk skirts or dresses.

After his toilet completed,
he'd lie down on the bed,
ask to be penetrated, only

if there were a man in the house.

PAST LIVES WHILE TAKING SELFIES FOR GRINDR

At the mirror, I am Anastasia,
                    unable
              to hold the phone
                    steady.
In another life,
          letters took
        weeks to reach,
              envelopes
        and pants waited
                to be opened.
It's not that I don't admire
                myself,
        more so, will he
                admire me?
These sunken cheeks,
                    my average dick?
        I have to ask
                these questions
            in between
            pretending to be
        the last *true* queen.
The resemblance is uncanny:
                    the blank stare,
              the ice seeping up
            through fogged lens,
                    who I say I am.

holy shit what a title

TALLAHASSEE RAIN

There's a moment you can't escape: the water
filling up streets, the men in the back bar, needing water.

He's taking a piss next to me. *Stare at the ceiling.*
You want to kiss it. Don't look. Just listen to the water.

I'll find this flood folded into a junk drawer, dance
feeling myself up with leftover bath water.

Just once on the lips, drunk. Things I remember:
hand wrapped hips, kitchen slow dance, boiling water.

I could kaleidoscope his face: facets staring back,
cinderblock his feet, my hands holding him under water.

Colin always watched from the bathroom doorway. My pants
halfway down my legs, arm outstretched to test the water.

COLIN BECOMES A STAG

*

some nights he would wear
a pair of antlers

do a little dance

over the bed
his ass

hanging out
of his underwear

*

but the deer had spread

trash across the lawn

the pie plates

danced all over

*

last time he was a man
he leapt from bed

before dawn

the flash of white
tail off

through the dark

Soft Mouth

My mouth wet with dreams of cantaloupe
stacks at the supermarket.

Where he bit between my ribs, pressed
the bottom to check ripeness.

A hunting dog drags ducks,
fresh dead, from the swamp.

Somewhere a man crushed a man.
Pebbles no bigger than a tongue

traced the weakest spot, bowed
legs with sweetness.

SHERIDAN RAIN

We don't know
the touch of light
breaking through blinds.
It isn't morning, you can't walk
away. The choirs in my head sing,
                              No.
We know what Mozart said:
                              1451.
A tire swing, it comes back around
faster, faster,
                    you need another master.
Write down all the songs you know by
heart. Invisible fishing string
breaks the White River
before you're through the door,
coffee steam filling the house.

Yes, it's time to get up.
Sure, I'll walk your car to the end
of the driveway. Pebbles stuck
in bare feet. All the things
I couldn't—

I haven't been barefoot
on gravel road since that summer
my hands found your hips.

All the bandages I would need,
just to watch you go.

COLIN ON I-35

Colin forces himself into
the backseat of another Jeep,
like the cattle Colins pass on the way

to The City. Tonight it's Phoenix
where everyone is new,
has another name,

forget ear tag number,
just kiss it, there will be breakfast
in bed, or a note that *says it was great*

have a good time in the city or
a moment after the little death
that says *leave*, or maybe

Colin gets lassoed at Round Up,
the cowboy type who wants
a wife. Statistically,

everyone bases love
off of their first.
This is true if you close one

eye and say all Colins loud
enough that everyone forgets
who sings the song and thinks

Colin sang it first.
If Colin considers absolutes,
data excesses equal loneliness.

There are only so many cattle
that fit into a truck,
only so much weight can be

dragged off to slaughter.

II

THE BOOK OF COLIN

*

Two Colins arrived in the evening,
and Colin waited in the gateway.

When he saw them, he got up,
bowed his face to the ground.

Colin can wash his feet here,
Colin can go on his way in the morning.

Colin can find Colin leaning out
the window without shirt sleeves.

Colin, what is left
of the night?

*

These Colins burn whatever
they do not understand.

Destroyed, like ash
knows gravity, abandon

themselves to error
for the sake of sex.

They feast without fear, waterless
clouds carried along

the winds; become fall trees falling
without fruit, twice dead, uprooted.

*

Colin dreams of coral
islands. The breath between

stone walls is restless
wind around his throat

and Alexandria is always
on fire. Choke out all

the unsayable
syllables. Like Greek,

Colin loves anywhere
there is not a name for Colin.

Holy. Shit.

*

Because he is neither warm
nor cold, Colin must leave

Colin's house, stand outside,
knock till someone opens

a door in heaven.
The first voice Colin heard

was Colin. As if it were
a trumpet saying, *come*

*I will show things which must be
hereafter.*

*

Colin set the tables,
Colin spread the rugs.

Colin eat, Colin drink.
Get up, oil the fields!

When Colin sees chariots
with teams of horses, riders

on donkeys, or riders
on camels, let him be

fire, alert,
fully Colin.

SONG

To give up means kiss.
There isn't
a garden, just a street
lined with Bradford Pears
that don't yield pears,
just flowers. It's deceiving.
Flowers on flowers on flowers,
you said *love looks like this*.
What we pile on graves
means everything. Repetition,
like supermarket mirrors,
infinite temporality. I want
a real pear, 2 for a dollar
and tender, gritty against
teeth, space between
wake and sleep.

THE HEART IS A SHOTGUN HOUSE

*

no hall

three rooms
rubbing up against
each other

a house without
a backdoor

in the living room
smell every spice

the pots
boiling over

the wind
through the bedroom
window

*

we made moonshine
in the bath

put all the bottles
on the front lawn

to bathe them
in moonlight

left the tap
running

kissed

on the porch

*

I caught him eating
leftover spiced apples
in the midnight kitchen

after sleeping
with a shotgun

you'll pull the trigger

aim for anything
in the dark

HOOK ECHO

wherever hand meets
you arch away
say *build a bridge*

here is a bridge

I know the curve,
your back in sleep
a dry creek
you say *find a new stream*

here is a stream

if you wait
that means something

if you cast pebbles
that means something

I know the weight of glass
your hand weeping
in Texas heat

they say *send
him a drink*

here is your drink

if I open the cellar door
that means something

if the sky looks like split soup
that means something

if a tornado touches town
you can hide

here

SCHOOL FOR THE BLIND

Everyone learns to kiss
in a high
        school parking lot.
It's hard to practice, dropping
      you off to teach,
among people.
         Boys and men
wandering with white
    sticks.

Once, in a bar a man found my chest with a bat.

When the blind pass, gravity
   still pulls.
     my neck
  rising toward them
         black-cat angry, like hot asphalt.

I know they can't see us,
their eyes: tinted
        windows. I know
I have nothing
    to fear,   but still—

MAPS

*

Hallways demand running
the tiles spaced out step

length. If only love
were easy, follow you

down three feet till
a doctor says *you can't*

be here. As if anyone
could explain why

you were falling, like
anyone would fall apart,

as if anyone would acknowledge
the one person asking

for you.

*

Mercator making-out with Atlas
means one of two things:

1. This is Colin Halloween
2. This is Halloween

Everything depends on decades,
whether the ocean is flat

or crossable. Run around
a circle, you'll end up here.

Run around the inevitable
and you'll end up with shotgun

regret. Run around singing love
and you'll fall off the face

of the Earth.

*

Country song: all the roads
you took lead back to abandon,

the moment I miss
biting your bicep flesh.

This is sweet meat no one
can find without my taste,

sense of the sheets
and how they pile in rivers

made for tracing. North
says right. Estuary says

love; the source of all
understanding is wet

with manifest want.

*

Someone says something about a city
where I can love you. Mirrored

streets always wet with rain.
Where everything is beautiful

and nothing hurts. Where everything
is, nothing hurts. Like over

the river, some one always
screams. If there is any forgiveness

I'll walk Virginia. Memphis, give me
stones, Louisville give me

love, Stone Mountain let me
look out beyond, Little Rock

let me speak.

NEW RECIPE

You wanted tomatoes, red.
Caprese salad, mozzarella

firm yet tender. To divide
basil into sections, you

need a chef's knife.
The only thing you know

about cutting:
you can't return to

new. Like flesh and blood,
over the kitchen sink,

petaling down your thumb.

ETYMOLOGY OF COLIN

*

In a new office, Colin can't
say his name, pulls his socks up too far,
says nothing. What anyone cares
about Colin is the job
that gets the job done.

*

Some things can't be undone:
crack in the dam,
jump from the side
of the pool.
You can't take back.

*

Everyone wants similarity, symmetry,
two trees at the end of the drive
like home. Colin's father is named Colin,
his grandfather is named Colin,
but they are not—

*

Hands up
and down every inch,
there are too many stairs
to say something,
you can't reverse.

*

The park where Colin's
step-dad says *tell me you are not Colin*!
Swing chains shaking,
Colin is thirteen.
Someone should love Colin for being
                                        Colin.

*

Colin tells his grandfather about Colin
and finds his baby pictures
in the burn barrel before
he heads back to the sticks:
you can't unburn.

THE STORY RETOLD WITH ALL
THE RIGHT PLAYERS

To be on fire,
to be forever,

                    means to burn.

Chest deep in river
        we were made
    of stars, July dancing
           across your skin.
The things we'd give up:
       picket fence, doctor visits,
           sitting next to each other
    in church.

     The water fills my mouth
   to wash the whispers out.
There isn't enough soap
            for silence.

      We could have lived without –
but chose alchemy.
      What you want must be
  equal to what you give.
In German the words for love and life
differ by one vowel
       Lieben und leben.

    I've seen it in the flights of birds
I've seen it in you, the upturned
     bellies of fish along the river.

Nothing can last in its natural state, except a story
where we meet in the morning.

      Two boys
                              walk with pockets full of stones
      through the town square,
down to the river.

III

On Meeting You

bodies in motion

and then you

I didn't believe in
music of the spheres

way

my body sank
into surrounding space

how I was
heavier toward you

COLIN IS CHANGING HIS NAME

*

There's the way it will never
work. The boots
                to the chest,
the crosses, park benches,
cross roads, where no one is
meant to meet,
               only go. On Sunday
Colin can't love another Colin. Don't hold hands
    except in prayer.
Colin's family might be okay with another Colin,
It all depends.

    Ask Colin's parents if
            they trust you with Colin,
   if Colin is a prize,
         if you can just take Colin,
   if Colin wants to be taken. It's better to just take him
and run,
    but sometimes Colins feel the need to ask.
So much depends
     upon Colin.

*

Figure out who goes
                    first:
        everyone says to not
                    take Colin out on the river
            at moonlight,
sing songs that beg for kisses
                    and clichés. Everyone   knows
        to not knock him up
unless they want Smith
                    and Wesson escort.
 Everyone knows
        rings should be worth
        so many months
                    it hurts.
Only Colin knows
        when you ask what to do on your knees,
it must mean
                    something.

*

Do it in a forest,
    a gay bar,
after class when no one
    can hear you say *love*.
        To two boys
    who just want
    to hold hands,

there are too many maps
to be made.

      Kiss his neck at the Restless Wind.
Clutch the curve of his back
       in the parking lot of the Mad
    Butcher. Sway back and forth on the south green
of his college,
      the trees made fire in spring,
     Christmas lights forgotten for this night.

Say something
    French. Maybe a film,
       better yet, dinner. Lobster
  or red, anything
you want to tell everyone most. The corner
    of Fourth and Hester
where you met, meant
    everything.

[Handwritten annotation:] I ran out of blue pens but all these lines are my fuckin favorite lines HOLY SHIT!

SLOW TESTAMENT
June 26ᵗʰ, 2015

How cliché to say *Cicada*
song and mean White River
where summer air breathes
like roux, every note echoes off

Jon boats. I want to say your name
like it's mine, familiar and bitter
as chicory, no toothbrush can
brush out, carry the taste like
secret in my mouth all day.

Say *honey* and mean *vertebrae*

gilded in sunshine and scalloped
like a tissue paper paged book
meant for finding where I left
off quick, when the song kicks

back in after the silence that being
watched brings. We've lived
too long among roots to not
sing the hymn of surviving
the work of breaking

out of your own flesh.

NOTES

"Pyschopathia Sexualis" is a found poem that is based on accounts of homosexual men in Richard Von Kraft-Ebing's *Pyschioathia Sexualis*. The numbers correspond directly to their descriptions.

"The Book of Colin" is based on the story of "Sodom and Gomorrah," and the Book of Revelation (King James Version) along with Bob Dylan's "All Along the Watchtower."

Acknowledgments

I am grateful to the following journals and anthologies where some of these poems previously appeared:

Assaracus ("Sleepover"); *Burnt District* ("Zone of Silence"); *Ghost Ocean Magazine* ("Soft Mouth"); *Moon City Review* ("Tallahassee Rain"); *Ninth Letter* ("Slow Testament"); *Pembroke Magazine* ("Hook Echo"); *The Queer South: LGBTQ Writers on the American South* ("Colin Becomes a Stag" and "Things Come Back"); *Redivider* ("Approaching Infinity"); *Short, Fast, and Deadly* ("On Meeting You")

Special thanks to my mentors, Lisa Lewis, Sandy Longhorn, and Kathleen Pierce, for their support and guidance on my path to this book. I'd also like to thank my friends, colleagues, and peers at the University of Central Arkansas, Texas State University, and Oklahoma State University for the camaraderie, mischief, and time spent together. Finally, I'd like to thank every "Colin" I've ever known for the inspiration of this book. You're in here, I promise.

ABOUT THE ARTIST

Bradley Phillips is an Assistant Professor of Photography at Southeast Missouri State University. In addition Bradley is the Multimedia Coordinator at Catapult Creative House, a creative arts incubator in Cape Girardeau, Missouri. He received his Master of Fine Arts in Visual Studies from the State University of New York at Buffalo and his Bachelors in Photography from Brooks Institute in Santa Barbara California. A selection of magazine and journals on which his work has appeared includes: *Creative Quarterly*, *The Big Muddy*, *The Cape Rock Review*, and the *Cimarron Review*. Bradley has exhibited his work nationwide, most notably at Art Space and CEPA Gallery in New York. More information about Bradley and his work can be found on his website, www.bradley-phillips.com.

ABOUT THE POET

John Andrews was born in Roseville, California, but grew up in Sheridan, Arkansas. His poems have appeared in *Assaracus*, *Burnt District*, *Columbia Poetry Review*, *Redivider*, *Pembroke Magazine*, and elsewhere. His poems have also been anthologized in *The Queer South: LGBTQ Writers on the American South* and *Aim For The Head: An Anthology of Zombie Poetry*. John holds a B.A. in Writing from the University of Central Arkansas and an M.F.A. from Texas State University where he was named a C.D. Marshall Creative Writing Fellow and served as managing editor for *Front Porch Journal*. He has taught creative writing and composition at Northern Oklahoma College, Oklahoma State University, and Texas State University. Also, he has taught K-12 students with Arkansas Governor's School, Austin Bat Cave, and Upward Bound. Currently, he lives in Stillwater, Oklahoma, with his fiancé where he is a Ph.D. student in English and Creative Writing at Oklahoma State University and serves as an Associate Editor for the *Cimarron Review*.

ABOUT THE PRESS

Sibling Rivalry Press is an independent press based in Little Rock, Arkansas. It is a sponsored project of Fractured Atlas, a nonprofit arts service organization. Contributions to support the operations of Sibling Rivalry Press are tax-deductible to the extent permitted by law, and your donations will directly assist in the publication of work that disturbs and enraptures. To contribute to the publication of more books like this one, please visit our website and click *donate*.

Sibling Rivalry Press gratefully acknowledges the following donors, without whom this book would not be possible:

TJ Acena

Kaveh Akbar

John-Michael Albert

Kazim Ali

Seth Eli Barlow

Virginia Bell

Ellie Black

Laure-Anne Bosselaar

Dustin Brookshire

Alessandro Brusa

Jessie Carty

Philip F. Clark

Morell E. Mullins

Jonathan Forrest

Hal Gonzlaes

Diane Greene

Brock Guthrie

Chris Herrmann

JP Howard

Shane Khosropour

Randy Kitchens

Jørgen Lien

Stein Ove Lien

Sandy Longhorn

Ed Madden

Jessica Manack

Sam & Mark Manivong

Thomas March

Telly McGaha & Justin Brown

Donnelle McGee

David Meischen

Ron Mohring

Laura Mullen

Eric Nguyen

David A. Nilsen

Joseph Osmundson

Tina Parker

Brody Parrish Craig

Patrick Pink

Dennis Rhodes

Paul Romero

Robert Siek

Scott Siler

Alana Smoot Samuelson

Loria Taylor

Hugh Tipping

Alex J. Tunney

Ray Warman & Dan Kiser

Ben Westlie

Valerie Wetlaufer

Nicholas Wong

Anonymous (18)

CPSIA information can be obtained
at www.ICGtesting.com
Printed in the USA
LVHW05s0717120418
573174LV00007B/51/P